101

Journal Questions

for Women.

*

TONY T ROBINSON.

Author, Tony T Robinson
Title, 101 Journal Questions for Women.

*

© 2015, Tony T Robinson

ISBN:9781515079347

DEDICATION.

*

I would like to dedicate this book to every woman who keeps a journal or who enjoys creative writing because I believe it can truly be a healing and cathartic experience. It is also one of the best ways to truly get to know yourself and understand and process your thoughts and feelings in a safe and constructive way.

To my friends and family and to those who have supported me along the way I am truly grateful.

*

Other books by

Tony T Robinson.

*

Self-esteem Affirmation Workbook & Journal.

*

101 Self Discovery Journal Prompts.

*

101 Quick and Easy Confidence Quotes.

*

101 Confidence Quotes that will change your life.

*

101 I AM Power Affirmations.

*

About this book.

*

I have written several books within the self-help/ self-development genre but each one is different and has a unique purpose whether that incorporates the use of Affirmations and Confidence Building Quotes or Journal prompts.

This is the second journal I have written. My last book "101 Self-Discovery Journal Prompts" focused on using a daily "trigger" word that encouraged the writer to explore their immediate reactions thereby uncovering unconscious thoughts and feelings that may otherwise have remained hidden. In this book I have provided very specific questions that may require some thoughtful consideration, they cover a wide spectrum of everyday life from relationships with partners and parents to self-esteem related questions.

I have tried to keep this book balanced by making sure that not all of the questions require you to dig "too deep" or go to a "Dark" place. There are other books with random journal prompts that are light hearted but I won't be asking you write a list of your favourite television programs or the name of your first pet.

I want to push you, I want you to dig deeper and explore your past and present and think about your dreams and desires. I want you to connect to a place of authenticity and if that requires some soul searching and a few tears along the way then so be it.

In my opinion keeping a journal is a very close companion to therapy and so it's the perfect place to pen your deepest thoughts and feelings. When you do that you have an opportunity explore and work through those feelings in a safe and constructive way without fear of criticism or rejection from others. There is nobody to tell you that you are right or wrong and nobody can invalidate how you feel.

I also want the experience to be pleasurable and fun so you can either work your way through this journal starting from the beginning one day at a time or you can flip through it and find whatever question feels like something you want to write about on that day.

A journal like this is possibly the best gift you can give to yourself but I also think it makes a perfect gift to give to your Mum, Sister, Daughter or friend and it can be something that you both work through together to make it a shared collaborative experience.

However you use this journal I hope you find it helpful and insightful and that it is a cathartic and healing process. I also hope it is empowering and self-esteem building.

You may know that I have several groups on Facebook but I have created a new group specifically for people who are using my journals and workbooks. Therefore and just for fun I encourage you to take a photograph of yourself holding up the book and share it in the group, you can also add a message about what you like about the book or specific questions that you find enjoyable.

The group is called Affirmations Journals and Art Therapy and you are very welcome to join.

So with that said I will let you get on with it.

Much love Tony T.

1.

What makes you Happy?

2.

What are your top 10 achievements?

3.

What is the greatest lesson you have ever learnt?

4.

What is your greatest strength as a woman?

5.

What makes you smile?

What is your purpose in life?

7.

What does the word Spirituality mean to you?

8.

Complete this sentence. I feel anxious when –

9.

In what ways are you selfless?

10.

In what ways are you selfish?

11.

Write a poem entitled there once was a girl called (add your name)

12.

When was the last time you cried and why?

13.

Describe your perfect partner.

14.

I am grateful for_________

15.

Do you find it hard to say NO to people and if so why?

Tomorrow will be a good day because______________

17.

What do you want most out of life?

18.

What does the word Happiness mean to you?

19.

If you could be anyone else in the world who would it by and why?

20.

What is your most embarrassing moment?

21.

List your best qualities.

22.

Do you take yourself too seriously? In what ways could you lighten up and give yourself a break?

23.

Is your glass half full or half empty?

24.

Do you feel in control of your life?

25.

What did you achieve today?

26.

What does money mean to you?

27.

If you were going to write a book what would it be about?

If you could ask God anything what would you ask?

29.

The nicest thing my Mum ever said to me was ___

Make a promise to yourself. I PROMISE________________

I PROMISE TO LOVE MYSELF MORE

31.

What motivates you?

32.

If you could change one thing about your appearance today what would it be and why?

33.

If you were a man what do you think you would be like.

What do you wish your parent/s would have said to you growing up or as an adult that they never said?

35.

What are you most Proud of?

36.

What is your best character trait?

37.

What are you most scared of.

What did you accomplish today?

39.

In what ways do you compare yourself to other women?

Who are you most Jealous of and why?

41.

List one goal that you want to achieve in the next month.

Do you find it difficult to put yourself first and if so why?

43.

Keep a list of all of the positive thoughts you had today.

44.

What do you want out of life?

45.

What is the greatest obstacle you have ever overcome?

What's in your handbag that you really need to get rid of?

NOTHING

MY PURSE IS REALLY SMALL — I'VE ALWAYS LOVED SMALL PURSES. RIGHT NOW IT HOLDS MY CHANGE-PURSE-STYLE WALLET, PHONE, LIP BALM, A LIPSTICK OR TWO, BREATH SPRAY & A PEN. IT ALSO HAS SOME PAPERS IN IT... ONE I WANT TO LEAVE ~~AT HOME~~ IN MY CAR, UNTIL THERAPY TO TRY FIGURE OUT MY BILL, SO THERE SOMETHING TO TAKE OUT OF MY PURSE & LEAVE IN MY CAR.

I COULD REMOVE A FEW PENS

47.

What is your ideal job?

Once upon a time there was a young girl called

___________and ______

49.

What is your happiest memory?

If you could ask your Mother one question what would it be?

51.

If you could ask your Father one question what would it be?

52.

How clean is your Karma?

53.

What would your perfect day look like?

54.

What is your biggest insecurity?

55.

What makes you a good friend? Are there ways you can be a better friend.

What is the soul and what do you think yours look like?

57.

What is your biggest regret?

58.

In what ways are you judgemental and how could you be more compassionate?

59.

What can you do to be healthier and fitter?

60.

What does the word "Worthy" mean to you?

61.

How worthy do you feel?

Make a list of all of your successes.

63.

When do you feel lonely and why?

What is your favourite swear word. Make it fill the page.

65.

Is there a specific personality trait that you need to work on?

How do you act or react when you are upset?

67.

What advice would you give your teenage self?

STOP WORRYING ABOUT WHAT OTHER PEOPLE THINK. YOUR MOM & DAD ARE GREAT PEOPLE — AND THEY DON'T GET EVERYTHING RIGHT. THEY ARE PASSING THEIR ISSUES ON TO YOU — ~~STO~~ STOP ABSORBING EVERYTHING. ITS OK TO HAVE A MIND OF YOUR OWN

LOVE SHOULDN'T HAVE TO BE EARNED, IT SHOULD BE FREELY GIVEN TO YOU. YOU DON'T HAVE TO EARN GODS LOVE

YOU ARE NOT FAT

YOU ARE GOOD ENOUGH EXACTLY AS YOU ARE. YOU DON'T NEED TO CHANGE A THING.

YOU DON'T HAVE TO TRY SO HARD OR PROOVE ANYTHING

BE NICE TO YOURSELF.

Are you afraid of failure? What constitutes failure to you?

69.

What makes you sad?

If you could be any animal what would you be and why.

71.

How do you feel or react when someone criticises you?

In what ways are you or have you been bitchy and why do you think you behave that way?

73.

Whose standards do you measure yourself against and why?

Decide on what is good enough for you.

How do you want to be remembered after you have passed away?

75.

Write down one of your naughtiest fantasies.

What do you add/bring to your relationships?

77.

If you had more time for yourself how would you spend it? – How can arrange or rearrange your life to accommodate this desire.

Do you have any apologies that you need to make to anyone but never have. If so write them here?

79.

Do you hold onto anger, if so why and what can you do to let it go?

Write a letter to someone that you miss. (It's just for you, you don't have to send it.)

81

What do you most need to attract into your life?

82.

What is the biggest lie you have ever told?

83.

In what ways can you be kinder to yourself?

84.

What did your childhood teach you?

85.

What makes you happy?

How do you deal with change, do you think you are adaptable?

87.

What was your last dream?

88.

What things in life give you the most fulfilment?

89.

What is the newest and oldest item of clothing in your wardrobe?

90.

Where would you like to be in ten years' time?

91.

What was your favourite holiday and why.

Write a List of reasons why you are amazing.

93.

If you could do anything secretly that nobody would ever find out about what would you do?

94.

What do you like about yourself the most?

95.

Complete this sentence. I am a strong woman because –

Write a list of words to describe yourself.

97.

If you had ten wishes what would they be?

What would you do if you won the lottery?

- BUY A HOUSE ON A BEAUTIFUL BEACH
- WORK LESS – PROBABLY IN A CONSULTING ROLE
- BE MORE ACTIVE – BIKING & YOGA
- PAY OFF ALL MY NEICES STUDENT LOANS

99.

Describe your perfect date.

100.

Give yourself 5 Compliments.

101.

Do you think you have learnt anything new about yourself while writing in this journal?

NOTES.

NOTES.

51565710R00065

Made in the USA
Lexington, KY
27 April 2016